George Eliot

D0619110

Very Interesting People

VIP

Bite-sized biographies of Britain's most fascinating historical figures

George Eliot

Very Interesting People

Rosemary Ashton

OXFORD
UNIVERSITY PRESS

OXFORD
UNIVERSITY PRESS

Great Clarendon Street, Oxford ox2 6DP

Oxford University Press is a department of the University of Oxford.
It furthers the University's objective of excellence in research, scholarship,
and education by publishing worldwide in

Oxford New York

Auckland Cape Town Dar es Salaam Hong Kong Karachi
Kuala Lumpur Madrid Melbourne Mexico City Nairobi
New Delhi Shanghai Taipei Toronto

With offices in

Argentina Austria Brazil Chile Czech Republic France Greece
Guatemala Hungary Italy Japan Poland Portugal Singapore
South Korea Switzerland Thailand Turkey Ukraine Vietnam

Oxford is a registered trade mark of Oxford University Press
in the UK and in certain other countries

Published in the United States
by Oxford University Press Inc., New York

First published in the *Oxford Dictionary of National Biography* 2004
This paperback edition first published 2007

© Oxford University Press 2007

Database right Oxford University Press (maker)

First published 2007

British Library Cataloguing in Publication Data

Data available

Library of Congress Cataloging in Publication Data

Data available

Typeset by SPI Publisher Services, Pondicherry, India
Printed in Great Britain
on acid-free paper by
Ashford Colour Press Ltd, Gosport, Hants.

ISBN 978-0-19-921351-1 (Pbk.)

10 9 8 7 6 5 4 3 2 1

Contents

Preface

The first problem to confront a biographer of George Eliot is what to call her. Born Mary Anne Evans, she chose the name Marian when she arrived in London in 1851, aged thirty-one, with the intention of making her way as a journalist and translator. In 1854 her relationship with the married G. H. Lewes became public; she now called herself Marian Evans Lewes, whereupon many of her contemporaries refused to accept her unorthodox situation and cut her acquaintance. *Scenes of Clerical Life*, her first fiction under the pseudonym George Eliot, appeared in 1858. In 1880, two years after Lewes's death, she married the younger John Cross, resuming her original first names, Mary Ann, until her death only a few months after the marriage.

Early biographers, including John Cross himself and even the liberal-minded Leslie Stephen, who wrote the appreciative account of her life—under the name Mary Ann Cross—in the *Dictionary of Biography* (1888), were embarrassed by the social stigma attached to her. They concentrated on the celebrity she achieved especially after the publication of *Middlemarch* in 1871–2, deliberately understating or omitting many details of her younger life, particularly her early years in London. It is possible now to discuss George Eliot's life without constraint and with the benefit of her unexpurgated letters, edited by the late American scholar Gordon S. Haight, and the diaries of her first employer (and possible lover) the radical publisher John Chapman, owner of the *Westminster Review*, which she edited with him. The circle she moved in during the 1850s was made up of some of the leading—or soon to be leading—writers and thinkers of the Victorian age: Charles Dickens, T. H. Huxley, Charles Darwin, Herbert Spencer. A modern account of her life can call her Marian Evans and take note, without embarrassment, of the unusualness, for the time, not only of her domestic situation but also of her intellectual life as an equal among such illustrious male contemporaries.

In this study, originally written for the new *Oxford Dictionary of National Biography*, I hope to bring into focus the unusual qualities George Eliot possessed in addition to that of shocking her contemporaries with her private arrangements—her learnedness, her command of several languages, her move away from orthodox religion, her interest in philosophy, science, history, and English and European literature. My aim, too, is to show the continuity of her intellectual, imaginative, and narrative skills from her early letters and reviews to the novels themselves.

Rosemary Ashton

August 2006

About the author

Rosemary Ashton is Quain Professor of English Language and Literature at University College London. Her books include critical biographies of George Eliot (1996) and Thomas and Jane Carlyle (2002), and a study of radical publishing, *142 Strand: A Radical Address in Victorian London* (2006).

Early life

Marian Evans [pseud.George Eliot] (1819–1880), novelist, was known under several names during her life: Mary Anne Evans (at birth), Mary Ann Evans (from 1837), Marian Evans (from 1851), Marian Evans Lewes (from 1854), and Mary Ann Cross (1880).

She was born Mary Anne Evans on 22 November 1819 at South Farm on the Arbury estate in the parish of Chilvers Coton, Warwickshire, the third child of the second marriage of Robert Evans (1773–1849), manager of the large estates of the Newdigate family of Arbury Hall. Robert Evans's work on the estate was wide-ranging. He not only surveyed land and buildings, managed relations with the tenant farmers on the estate, collected rents, oversaw repairs, and arranged the buying and selling of land, but was also involved in negotiations with road builders and coalmining businesses in the area. His journals and correspondence with Francis Newdigate show Evans to have been an inventive and inconsistent speller, but a man of integrity and determination, and one in whom his employer invested a great deal of trust and authority. The eponymous hero of George Eliot's first full-length novel, *Adam Bede* (1859), is based in some respects—particularly in regard to his pride in his work and his determination of character—on Robert Evans.

Robert Evans's first wife, Harriet Poynton, with whom he had a son, Robert (1802–1864), and a daughter, Fanny (1805–1882), died in 1809. In 1813 he married Christiana Pearson (1788?–1836), the daughter of a local farmer. The children of this marriage were Christiana, known as Chrissey (1814–1859), Isaac (1816–1890), and Mary Anne, the youngest, born in 1819. Twin sons were born in March 1821, but survived only a few days.

In the spring of 1820, when Mary Anne was only a few months old, the family moved from South Farm to a house known as Griff, situated just off the main road between Nuneaton and Coventry. This was her home until she was twenty-one. It was a large house with stables and outbuildings, a dairy and farmyard, and an orchard. In her semi-autobiographical sketch, 'Looking backward', found in her last published work, *Impressions of Theophrastus Such* (1879), George Eliot describes her native country as 'fat central England' with its elms, buttercups, and tree-studded hedgerows, but she remembers also the coalmining, the building of roads and railways, the cutting of canals to carry the coal from the mines. It was not all lush, rural, idyllic; many of the local villagers worked in the pits and lived in poor cottages on the Newdigate estate, and some of the tenant farmers experienced conditions of poverty rather than plenty. It was this varied nature of the rural life of her childhood that she later drew on for her novels, having as a child noticed the contrast between the lives of the tenants and that of the landed family at the magnificent Arbury Hall, where she was allowed, as a clever and serious schoolgirl, to browse in the family library.

The young evangelical

At five Mary Anne boarded with Chrissey at Miss Lathom's school in nearby Attleborough; in 1828, when she was nine, she became a boarder at Mrs Wallington's school in Nuneaton. Here she came under the strong religious influence of an evangelical teacher, Maria Lewis, to whom most of her earliest extant letters—earnest, pious, and rather self-righteous—are addressed. From thirteen to sixteen she attended a school in Coventry run by Mary and Rebecca Franklin, the daughters of a Baptist minister. Religious dissent was strong in the midlands at this time; there were chapels of all denominations: Baptist, Wesleyan, Unitarian, Quaker, Congregationalist. Though her own family belonged to the middle-of-the-road Anglican community, Mary Anne herself was strongly evangelical. As a teenager she alarmed her brother Isaac by taking her piety to extremes, frowning on theatregoing and neglecting her appearance—going about 'like an owl', as she said, 'to the great disgust of my brother' (Cross, 1.157).

At the Franklins' school Mary Anne won prizes in French and in English composition, and was known for her fine piano playing. Her schoolfellows later remembered her as a serious, clever girl, but a shy and sensitive one, who hated performing in public, and who often ran out of the room in tears. At Christmas 1835, when she was just sixteen, Mary Anne came home to a domestic crisis. Her mother, who had been in poor health since the death of the twins, was dying painfully of breast cancer.

After her mother's death in February 1836, Mary Anne stayed at home to help her sister Chrissey keep house. Her brother Isaac was now helping his father with the estate business, and would eventually take over from him, working for the next generation of the Newdigate family. In May 1837 Chrissey married Edward Clarke, a doctor in nearby Meriden. Mary Anne was bridesmaid, and when signing the register after the wedding, she dropped the 'e' from her forename. She now became housekeeper for her father and her brother Isaac. Although her schooling had ended with her mother's death and the assumption of domestic duties, she had continued to read widely and had lessons at home in Italian and German from a visiting tutor, Joseph Brezzi. She also read, under Maria Lewis's guidance, improving works such as the life of William Wilberforce.

Isaac married in 1841, and it was decided that he and his wife, Sarah, should live at Griff. Robert Evans retired as agent to the Newdigates, and he and Mary Ann found another house. In March 1841 they moved to a comfortable house in Foleshill, on the outskirts of Coventry. Perhaps Robert Evans hoped that his youngest daughter would find a suitable husband in Coventry despite her plain looks and serious demeanour. Instead, she made a new set of friends who were to have an important influence on her future life.

Mary Ann Evans's piety at the age of twenty was remarkable even in an age of pious evangelicalism among the provincial middle and lower classes. The correspondence between her and Maria Lewis was serious, preoccupied with religious matters, and somewhat sentimental. Mary Ann christened Miss Lewis Veronica, signifying 'fidelity in friendship', and was in turn given the name Clematis, which meant, appropriately enough, 'mental beauty'. In their correspondence they discussed their reading, mostly of religious and morally edifying works. One such letter, written by Mary Ann in March 1841, ends with a paragraph full of earnest spiritual aspirations:

May we both in our diverse but I trust converging paths be upheld and guided by the staff of Divine consolation and the light of Divine Wisdom. How beautiful is the 63d Psalm. 'Because Thy loving kindness is better than life my lips shall praise thee. Thus will I bless thee while I live, I will lift up my hands in thy name, my soul shall be satisfied as with marrow and fatness, and my mouth shall praise thee with joyful lips' etc. I feel strongly reproved by this picture of entire satisfaction in God as a portion. (*Letters*, 1.82)

Like her semi-autobiographical fictional character Maggie Tulliver in *The Mill on the Floss*, Mary Ann eventually reacted against such extreme piety and saintliness. Her intellectual curiosity led her to read widely in non-religious literature: Shakespeare, Scott, Cervantes, Schiller, Thomas Carlyle. After the move in 1841 to Foleshill she also came under the influence of the attractive Bray family of Coventry.

Freethinking turn

Charles Bray (1811–1884) was a wealthy ribbon manufacturer, a progressive in politics, and a philanthropist who used his wealth to set up schools and to support hospitals, all with a view to improving the social conditions of the poor. He was a freethinker in religion, a robust and original man, who did not care what his neighbours thought of him. In his autobiography,

Phases of Opinion and Experience during a Long Life (1884), Bray remembered with pride how his large house, Rosehill, was a Mecca for radicals and intellectuals who enjoyed the 'free-and-easy mental atmosphere' and 'the absence of all pretension and conventionality' which prevailed there. According to him, 'Every one who came to Coventry with a queer mission, or a crotchet, or was supposed to be "a little cracked", was sent up to Rosehill' (Bray, 69–70).

Along with his quiet wife, Cara, herself inclined to piety but not an orthodox Christian, and Cara's sister and brother, Sara and Charles Hennell, Bray offered Mary Ann an intellectually challenging milieu. Already bookish and well read in several languages, she became interested in historical accounts of the Bible—one by Charles Hennell and several by German Biblical historians—which cast doubt on the accounts of miracles and on the supernatural elements in the gospels.

By the end of 1841, at the age of twenty-two, after reading, among other works of historical scholarship, Charles Hennell's *Inquiry Concerning the Origin of Christianity* (1838), Mary Ann had come to the view that Christianity was based on 'mingled truth and fiction' (*Letters*, 1.28). On 2 January 1842 she refused to go to church. Her action resulted in anger and silence on the part of her father, which lasted for some months. Her brother Isaac told her she was jeopardizing the family's good name by associating with Coventry radicals and infidels. He despaired of her ever finding a husband, now that she was adding unorthodox opinions to her plain appearance. Robert Evans almost turned his daughter out of the house, but eventually he relented, and from then on an uneasy truce existed between them. She continued to keep house for him until he died in 1849, trying to be a dutiful daughter, but reserving the right to hold her own opinions on the subject of religion and to continue her friendship with the Brays.

At Rosehill, Mary Ann met many liberal thinkers, including the social philosophers Herbert Spencer and Harriet Martineau, the social experimentalist

Robert Owen, the radical publisher John Chapman, and Ralph Waldo Emerson on his visits from America. At the end of 1843, when Charles Hennell married Rufa Brabant, it was arranged that Mary Ann should take over from Rufa the translation of David Friedrich Strauss's scholarly investigation of the gospels published in 1835–6, *Das Leben Jesu, kritisch bearbeitet* (*The Life of Jesus, Critically Examined*). Mary Ann was the obvious person to take on the task. She was the most learned member of the Bray–Hennell circle, having made a close study of the Bible, first as ardent evangelical, then as historical critic. And she knew German. In 1846 John Chapman published, in three volumes, her translation of this work, which painstakingly investigated the events of Christ's life as told in all four gospels and found them to be not historical, but mythological—the wished-for fulfilment of Old Testament prophecies. Mary Ann received £20 for her labours.

Chapman was also to publish *The Essence of Christianity* (1854), her second translation of a

German work demystifying scripture, Ludwig
Feuerbach's *Das Wesen des Christenthums* (1841).
The translation was the only work to be published
under her name, Marian Evans. Both Strauss, and,
more particularly, Feuerbach had an influence on
her own position, illustrated widely in her novels,
as a humanist for whom relations between people
have all the sanctity reserved in orthodox religion
for the relationship between the individual and
God.

Though still a serious young woman, inclined to
depression and self-doubt and painfully conscious
of her plain appearance, Mary Ann began to show
that she was not just formidably intelligent and
knowledgeable, but also sharp-witted and imaginatively gifted. In October 1846 Charles Bray
received a letter in which she gave evidence that
she possessed all the qualities required of a novelist: wit, wisdom, imagination, and an ability to
turn her own experience to good account fiction-
ally. She exploits with playful ease the hard intellectual labour, not without its *longueurs*, of translating Strauss's work in her description to Bray of

a (fictitious) visit from a Professor Bücherwurm
of Moderig University (Professor Bookworm of
Musty University):

> Down I came, not a little elated at the idea
> that a live professor was in the house, and, as
> you know I have quite the average quantity of
> that valuable endowment which spiteful people
> call assurance, but which I dignify with the
> name of self possession, you will believe that
> I neither blushed nor made a nervous giggle
> in attempting to smile, as is the lot of some
> unfortunate young ladies who are immersed in
> youthful bashfulness. (*Letters*, 8.13)

Professor Bücherwurm is, by his own account,
'a voluminous author—indeed my works already
amount to some 20 vols.—my last publication in
5 vols. was a commentary on the book of Tobit'.
He has come to England in search of a wife
who will double as the translator of his scholarly
works, and he is idiosyncratic enough to desire,
'besides ability to translate, a very decided ugliness of person and a sufficient fortune to supply
a poor professor with coffee and tobacco, and

an occasional draft of schwarzbier, as well as to contribute to the expenses of publication'. He expresses himself satisfied that Mary Ann fulfils these criteria, though he regrets that she has no beard, 'an attribute which I have ever regarded as the most unfailing indication of a strong-minded woman'.

Mary Ann tells Bray how delighted she was by this proposal, since she is desperate to be saved from the 'horrific disgrace of spinster-hood' and to be taken away from England. The letter turns her learning to light-hearted and witty account, and makes a brave joke about her plain looks and her anxiety that, at the age of nearly twenty-seven, she may not find a husband, as well as providing a shrewd preparatory sketch for Mr Casaubon in *Middlemarch*. Furthermore, her ability here to illustrate her story by means of allusions, analogies, and metaphors drawn from literature, science, religion, and history gives a foretaste of the distinctiveness of her gifts as a novelist with a truly remarkable range of reference.

Journalism in London

A change of name

The next few years were for Mary Ann a lonely and painful time. She had to nurse her father through a long illness, during which he was demanding and often ungrateful. She was exhausted, physically and emotionally, when he died on 31 May 1849. Robert Evans was buried in Chilvers Coton churchyard, next to his wife. His property was divided between his sons Robert and Isaac; Fanny and Chrissey, who had been given £1000 each when they married, received another £1000 in his will, as well as household items. Mary Ann was left £2000 in trust, a sum which, when invested, would yield about £90 a year in interest, not quite enough to live on without supplementary earnings, but enough to encourage her to consider living independently. She might have gone to live with her married brother Isaac, resigning herself to a life of plain sewing, playing the piano, and reading to her nephews and nieces in a household of conventional religious and social observance which was to her stiflingly narrow. But she knew that she and Isaac disagreed about everything: politics, religion, and the duties of younger sisters to obey their older brothers. Although she got on better with her sister Chrissey, married to Edward Clarke, a struggling doctor (who died in 1852), she had no wish to settle with Chrissey's family either.

While Mary Ann wondered what to do next, the Brays generously offered to take her with them on a trip to Switzerland and Italy. After six weeks of travelling, the Brays returned to England, leaving her in Geneva, where she bravely took lodgings and spent a winter trying out her new found independence, and taking stock. A sympathetic family, the D'Albert Durades, took her in as a paying guest. François D'Albert Durade, who later translated several of her novels into French, was an artist. He painted her portrait in February 1850, representing her as modest, pensive, long-faced, but pleasant looking. Mary Ann spent her time in Geneva reading, walking, learning mathematics, and continuing with a translation (never to be finished) of Spinoza's *Tractatus theologico-politicus* which she had begun during her father's illness.

When she returned to England in March 1850, Mary Ann had more or less made up her mind to move to London and pursue a career in journalism. A short stay with Isaac and his family at Griff, followed by a rather less painful visit to Chrissey at Meriden, convinced her that she could not make her home among them. The decision to move to London was a momentous one, and was accompanied by a change of name. She now called herself Marian Evans, and in January 1851 she took up lodgings in the Strand.

John Chapman and the
Westminster Review

Thanks to the Brays, Marian Evans had an imme-
diate entrée into the world of radical politics and
journalism, of free thinking, and in some cases
of free living too. The Chapman household at
142 Strand was itself a most unconventional one.
The four-storey building, looking over Somerset
House and the Thames at the back, was both the
workplace and the home of the publisher John
Chapman, who specialized in publishing works of
a left-wing or sceptical tendency. He had been
impressed by Marian's intellect and by her sta-
mina in completing the translation of Strauss. He
came to value these qualities even more when in
1851 he bought the great radical periodical, the
Westminster Review, first set up in the 1820s to
further the cause of political and social reform in
the long run-up to the Reform Act of 1832. Marian
Evans became, in effect, the editor of the *Review*,
as well as one of its best and most widely admired
reviewers.

On the upper floors of 142 Strand lived Chapman's family and a number of lodgers—mainly literary people whose books he published or who wrote for the *Westminster Review*. Chapman held Friday night parties, when writers gathered to talk about literature and politics of a mainly radical kind. It was through Chapman that Marian Evans met Herbert Spencer (1820–1903) and his friend, the critic George Henry Lewes (1817–1878), with both of whom she was to fall in love. But first she succumbed to the charms of Chapman himself. He was handsome, worldly, successful, and his admiration for her abilities flattered Marian. Chapman lived with his wife, Susanna, a woman fourteen years older than he was—Chapman was thirty in 1851—their two children, and the children's governess, Elisabeth Tilley, who was also Chapman's mistress.

Into this unusual household came Marian Evans, a provincial young woman of plain and earnest appearance but of strong will and strong passion. Over the next few months a comedy was played out, with Chapman arousing the jealousy of both his wife (who seems to have accepted the governess's role in their lives) and his mistress by the attention he gave to the new guest. He visited Marian Evans's room, where she played the piano for him and taught him German. They were caught holding hands. Mrs Chapman and Elisabeth joined forces to expel the interloper, sending her, literally, to Coventry, where she fled in tears to the Brays, upset by Chapman's assurances that he admired her mental beauty (Clematis again), but found her lacking in physical charm.

Sensibly, Marian abandoned all hopes of Chapman as a lover and—establishing a pattern which she was also to follow with Herbert Spencer—settled down to a friendly, professional relationship with him. The women at 142 Strand relented, and in the autumn of 1851 Chapman brought Marian back to London, where she began to guide him in the editorial department of the *Westminster Review*. He was the nominal editor, while she, from a mixture of diffidence, modesty, and fear of playing a public role, was happy to remain behind

the scenes, doing the work and letting Chapman
put his name to it.

Marian's social life blossomed in London. Some-
times accompanied by Chapman, she attended
lectures in geometry at the new Ladies' College
in Bedford Square, later renamed Bedford College. She also frequently walked across the Strand
to see plays put on at the Lyceum Theatre in
Catherine Street (now Aldwych). Among these
was *The Game of Speculation*, G. H. Lewes's successful adaptation of Balzac's *Mercadet*, which
opened at the Lyceum in October 1851 and ran for
ninety-four performances. It was in October 1851,
too, that Marian Evans first met Lewes. Chapman
introduced them on 6 October at William Jeffs's
bookshop in the Burlington Arcade. Marian
reported to the Brays that Lewes was 'a sort of
miniature Mirabeau in appearance', a reference to
his slight physique and plain looks (*Letters*, 1.367).

A remarkable young woman

Marian worked closely with Chapman on
the *Westminster Review* until 1854. She was

invaluable to him with her sharp brain, wide knowledge, willing labour, and ability to deal tactfully yet firmly with touchy contributors. Chapman himself lacked all these qualities, as one of the chief contributors and supporters of the *Review*, George Combe, pointed out to him. Combe was a well-known phrenologist, a practitioner of that 'science' by which character was to be read by feeling the contours of the head. In 1851 he felt Marian Evans's bumps at Bray's house, and concluded, 'she appeared to me the ablest woman I have seen', having 'a very large brain', and large bumps of 'concentrativeness', and 'love of approbation' (*Letters*, 8.27–8). He advised Chapman in December 1851 to 'use Miss Evans's tact and judgment as an aid to your own', continuing, 'She has certain organs large in her brain which are not so fully developed in yours, and she will judge more correctly of the influence upon other persons of what you write and do, than you will do yourself' (ibid., 8.33). On hearing three years later that Marian Evans had gone to Germany with the married G. H. Lewes, Combe was horrified.

He wrote to Bray in November 1854: 'I should like to know whether there is insanity in Miss Evans's family; for her conduct, with *her* brain, seems to me like morbid mental aberration' (ibid., 8.129).

Marian gained from the partnership with Chapman a widened social circle, the experience of running a review under cover of anonymity, the freedom to take decisions, and the chance to review works for the *Westminster* on topics ranging from English, French, and German literature to science to philosophy to evangelical sermons. Although at first she worked in return for board and lodgings at Chapman's house, from 1855 she was paid between £12 and £20 per article, earning between £60 and £120 per annum for her journalism (*Letters*, 7.358–9). She found her voice as a writer in her work for the *Westminster Review* from 1851 to 1856. In the essayist, increasingly confident, wide-ranging, witty, and rhetorically complex, we can see many of the characteristics of the future novelist George Eliot.

Marian Evans's social position as a single working woman in London in the early 1850s was extremely unusual. Generally, women of small means either married (whereupon their income promptly became their husbands' property under the law) or took jobs as governesses or live-in companions to rich relations or acquaintances. Marian herself had thought of becoming a teacher in Leamington Spa when her father threatened to make her leave the house in 1842, but had not relished the idea of becoming a domestic slave in a strange household or boarding establishment. On the other hand, there was a risk attached to cutting loose. Her brother disapproved of the move to London, making her feel that she would no longer be welcome in his home, even for visits. She was now in a society composed entirely of men, and though it was intellectually stimulating to associate with them freely, she was risking her reputation in doing so. She must often, too, have missed the companionship of a female friend in London, although she still corresponded with Cara Bray and Sara Hennell in Coventry.

In one letter to them in May 1852 Marian reported a great occasion at 142 Strand. On 4 May Chapman held a meeting of publishers, writers, and booksellers to protest against the Booksellers' Association, a cartel of larger publishers which fixed the price of books, prohibiting small publishers like Chapman from offering discounts. Dickens took the chair, 'preserving', according to Marian, 'a courteous neutrality of eyebrow, and speaking with clearness and decision' (*Letters*, 2.23). Many famous liberals and radicals were there: Herbert Spencer, Lewes, the scientist Richard Owen, Wilkie Collins, and many more distinguished men. Marian Evans was also there—the only woman.

Marian's position was a remarkable one, as several of her acquaintances noted. In 1885 William Hale White read the biography of George Eliot written by John Walter Cross (1840–1924), whom she had married in 1880, and was moved to write his recollection of Marian Evans, who had been his fellow lodger in the Strand in the early 1850s:

She was really one of the most sceptical, unusual creatures I ever knew, and it was this side of her character which was to me the most attractive…I can see her now, with her hair over her shoulders, the easy chair half sideways to the fire, her feet over the arms, and a proof in her hands, in that dark room at the back of No. 142, and I confess I hardly recognize her in the pages of Mr Cross's—on many accounts— most interesting volumes. I do hope that in some future edition, or in some future work, the salt and spice will be restored to the records of George Eliot's entirely unconventional life. (*The Athenaeum*, 28 Nov 1885)

Hale White was right. Cross took great liberties with his wife's letters, removing any phrases he thought controversial or compromising (*Letters*, 1.xiii). One wonders what Cross would have made of a letter to Chapman in February 1856, in which Marian vigorously urges him not to print in the *Westminster* an article by a Miss H on the French woman writer George Sand. She describes Miss H (Matilda Hays) as 'one of the numerous class of female scribblers who undertake to edify the public before they know the proper use of their own language'. The article is made up of 'feminine rant of the worst kind, which it will be simply fatal to the Review to admit' (Ashton, 'New George Eliot letters', 121–2). Further, 'I would not trust the most ordinary subject, still less the most delicate, to a woman who writes such trash'; and 'Everything she says about George Sand is undiscriminating Bosh'.

All of Marian's letters to Chapman about the conduct of the *Review* are like this, confident, wideranging, managerial, even magisterial towards her employer, the attractive, desirable, but intellectually inferior man of the world.

Relations with Herbert Spencer

This unconventional young woman, who had attended lectures, theatre, and opera during 1851 with Chapman, was soon going to the theatre and opera with Herbert Spencer. By June 1852 Marian was reporting to the Brays that she and

Spencer were seen so often in one another's company that 'all the world is setting us down as engaged' (*Letters*, 2.35). Marian would have liked nothing better, but Spencer was less keen. In July Marian went off alone to Broadstairs on holiday; from there she sent several managing letters to Chapman about the *Westminster Review*, careful letters to Combe, whom Chapman was pressing for money to help the *Review* out of a financial crisis, and, at the same time, love letters to Spencer. She wrote begging him to visit her at Broadstairs. All her passion and pride and humour are on display, as well as her loneliness and uncertainty:

Dear Friend

No credit to me for my virtues as a refrigerent. I owe them all to a few lumps of ice which I carried away with me from that tremendous glacier of yours. I am glad that Nemesis, lame as she is, has already made you feel a little uneasy in my absence, whether from the state of the thermometer [a reference to the very high temperatures that July] or aught else. We will not inquire too curiously whether you long most for my society or for the sea-breezes. If you decided that I was not worth coming to see, it would only be of a piece with that generally exasperating perspicacity of yours which will not allow one to humbug you. (An agreeable quality, let me tell you, that capacity of being humbugged. Don't pique yourself on not possessing it.) (ibid., 8.50–51)

Spencer did visit Marian briefly in Broadstairs and obviously discouraged her, for a week later she wrote again, almost proposing marriage to him:

Those who have known me best have always said, that if ever I loved any one thoroughly my whole life must turn upon that feeling, and I find they say truly. You curse the destiny which has made the feeling concentrate itself on you—but if you will only have patience with me you shall not curse it long. You will find that I can be satisfied with very little, if I am delivered from the dread of losing it. (*Letters*, 8.56–7)

Finally, she asserts her sense of self-worth, admitting that probably 'no woman ever before wrote such a letter as this', but insisting she is not ashamed, 'for I am conscious that in the light of reason and true refinement I am worthy of your respect and tenderness, whatever gross men or vulgar-minded women might think of me' (ibid., 8.57).

These letters to Spencer give some insight into how, when she came to write fiction, George Eliot could be so penetrating in her analyses of the complex relations between men and women, both those who marry and those—like Maggie Tulliver with Stephen Guest and Philip Wakem, or like Gwendolen Grandcourt with Daniel Deronda— who have intimate relationships which do not end in marriage.

Life with G. H. Lewes

Potential for scandal

By 1853 George Henry Lewes had replaced
Herbert Spencer in Marian Evans's affections, and
fortunately he returned them. He, too, was a regular contributor to the *Westminster Review*, as well
as theatre critic for *The Leader*, the weekly paper
which he co-edited with his friend Thornton
Hunt. Lewes, two years older than Marian, had
had a busy and varied career. From an insecure
background, brought up by his mother and a hated
stepfather, with a miscellaneous schooling, he had
worked his way to prominence in literary London
by means of prodigious talent, versatility, and hard
work.

When Marian Evans met Lewes in Jeffs's book-shop in October 1851 he was already the author of a popular history of philosophy; two novels; several plays and adaptations of French farces, some of which Marian saw at the Lyceum with Chapman or Spencer; a biography of Robespierre; and hundreds of articles and reviews. He was planning a life of Goethe. He had acted success-fully with Dickens's amateur theatre company, and had even toyed with the idea of going on the stage professionally. Like Marian he was fluent in French and German, and widely read in litera-ture, philosophy, and science. He had no religious faith. He was married and unable to sue for a divorce.

In February 1841 Lewes had married Agnes Jervis (1822–1902), the beautiful eighteen-year-old daughter of a radical MP, Swynfen Jervis. They had agreed to have an open marriage, the result of which was that in addition to having three surviving sons by Lewes, Agnes had by 1851 borne two children whose father was not Lewes, but his friend Thornton Hunt. She was to have two more children by Hunt in 1853 and 1857. Lewes, having entered on this open marriage, registered the first two of these children as his own. When he subsequently met and fell in love with Marian Evans, he could not sue for divorce, as under the terms of the law he had condoned his wife's adultery by registering the births of her children by Hunt in his own name. Though he was by 1853 disillusioned with his domestic arrangements—and notably did not register the birth of Agnes's daughter Ethel, born in October 1853—he had disqualified himself from ever seeking a divorce.

He had, however, left Agnes, probably in 1852, although he visited her and his children frequently at their home in Kensington, supported them financially, and was generous to Agnes for the rest of his life, as was Marian after his death. Agnes, who outlived them both by many years, living on until 1902, received amounts of between £100 and £250 per annum (Haight, *Biography*, 370, 460–61, 491). According to Marian's close friend Barbara Leigh Smith (later Mme

Bodichon), Lewes and Marian chose not to have children of their own (ibid., 205). Marian, who instinctively shrank from publicity and from scandal—though ironically the great decisions of her life involved her in both—did not want to bear children who would suffer from having parents who were not married.

Settling down

In October 1853 Marian moved to new lodgings at 21 Cambridge Street, Hyde Park Square, where she could receive Lewes less publicly than at 142 Strand. It has long been thought that their liaison dated from this move of hers, but it can be shown that they were probably intimate by the end of 1852 or beginning of 1853. In fact, it seems that Marian was already attracted to Lewes while she was still 'in love' with Spencer (Ashton, *Lewes*, 132–43). She knew from her own experience that it is possible to be confused in one's emotional life, and the heroines of George Eliot's novels are often in a state of doubt about their feelings. Maggie Tulliver, the most obviously autobiographical of them, certainly loves two men at once—or three, when one considers that her deepest feelings are those for her brother Tom. We can see something of a similar dilemma in Marian's life in the letters she wrote to the Brays during 1852–3.

Surprisingly perhaps, the Brays did not much like Lewes. Unorthodox though they were, they thought him bohemian, flippant, metropolitan, not quite respectable (though this showed some hypocrisy on Charles Bray's part, since he kept a mistress by whom he had a daughter, Elinor, whom he and Cara, who was childless, had adopted).

Throughout 1852 and early 1853 Marian was meeting Lewes regularly in the company of Spencer, with whom Lewes was friendly, and her letters to the Brays during the 'romance' with Spencer often mention Lewes too. In June 1852 the Brays were obviously trying to bring Spencer to the brink of a proposal to Marian. They invited Spencer to visit them in Coventry later that summer, when Marian would also be there.

Marian connived at the matchmaking. Lewes was also invited to visit, though not at the same time as Spencer. Marian's response was a rather excited and contradictory one:

> *Entre nous*, if Mr Lewes should not accept your invitation now, pray don't ask him when I am with you—not that I don't like him—*au contraire*—but I want nothing so Londonish when I go to enjoy the fields and hedgerows and yet more, friends of ten years' growth. (*Letters*, 2.37)

In the end, Marian visited the Brays alone at the end of October, having clarified her position with Spencer in Broadstairs in July. Meanwhile, she had been reading on this holiday Lewes's not very good novel *Rose, Blanche and Violet* (1848), and her letters from this point on have frequent references to his articles for the *Westminster* and his activities as theatre critic of his own weekly newspaper, *The Leader*. Soon she was going to the theatre with Lewes, not Spencer. On her thirty-third birthday, 22 November 1852, she wrote to the Brays describing her day. After lunch she had just got down to work when, 'with two clear hours before dinner, rap at the door—Mr Lewes—who of course sits talking till the second bell rings' (*Letters*, 2.68).

Marian found herself often defending Lewes against criticism. She told Cara Bray in April 1853 that Lewes was 'a man of heart and conscience wearing a mask of flippancy' (*Letters*, 2.98). In December 1853 she wrote a strong letter to Chapman, trying to get him to refuse an article by the new star on the scientific horizon, T. H. Huxley, in which Huxley attacked Lewes's book, *Comte's Philosophy of the Sciences*, praising Harriet Martineau's rival book, an abridged translation of Comte's work. Lewes's book had been published by Bohn, Martineau's by Chapman himself. Marian frankly advises Chapman to 'expunge' Huxley's review from the *Westminster*:

My opinion is, that the editors of the Review will disgrace themselves by inserting an utterly worthless & unworthy notice of a work by one

of their own writers—a man of much longer &
higher standing than Mr. Huxley, & whom Mr.
H's seniors in science & superiors both in intellect & fame treat with respect. (Ashton, 'New
George Eliot letters', 120)

In another letter written probably on the same
day, she added, 'Do you really think that if you had
been the publisher of Mr. Lewes's book and Bohn
the publisher of Miss Martineau's, Mr. Huxley
would have written just so? "Tell that to the
Marines"' (*Letters*, 2.133).

Literature and life

It was probably in late 1852 or early 1853 that
Marian and Lewes became lovers. Some time
in 1853 they reached a momentous decision—
more significant for her than for him—the decision to live together openly as man and wife.
Once more Marian Evans changed her name,
though not legally. From now on she called herself Mrs Lewes or Marian Evans Lewes. Although
it was not uncommon for Victorian men to have

mistresses—as Bray, Chapman, and Wilkie Collins did—such arrangements were usually kept quiet. This was different. Marian and Lewes made no secret of their liaison, which they considered a true marriage. Marian's reputation suffered most. As she wrote in September 1855 to her old friend Cara Bray, who at first could not bring herself to see Marian:

> Light and easily broken ties are what I neither
> desire theoretically nor could live for practic-
> ally. Women who are satisfied with such ties do
> not act as I have done—they obtain what they
> desire and are still invited to dinner. (*Letters*,
> 2.214.)

George Eliot often puts her heroines in difficult— even dangerous—emotional situations in which they attract criticism from society for breaking, or appearing to break, its social rules. Dorothea begins to love Will Ladislaw even while she is dutifully married to Mr Casaubon; it is a tribute to George Eliot's power as a writer, and her knowledge of human nature, that she per- suades us that Dorothea herself is unaware of her feelings for Ladislaw. She shows, of course, that Mr Casaubon himself is all too aware of the attraction between his young wife and his young cousin.

The Mill on the Floss, her most autobiographical novel in the portrayal of the childhood relationship between Tom and Maggie Tulliver, is also the novel in which George Eliot comes closest to describing prohibited relationships. Maggie falls in love with Stephen Guest against all her wishes and her sense of prior duties. They elope together, and then Maggie returns without consummating the affair, but to all appearances the fallen woman. George Eliot launches a strong attack on society's way of thinking the worst in relations between the sexes, pointing out how much harder public opinion is on the woman in such situations than on the man:

It was soon known throughout St. Ogg's that Miss Tulliver was come back: she had not, then, eloped in order to be married to Mr Stephen Guest—at all events, Mr Stephen Guest had not married her—which came to the same thing, so far as her culpability was concerned. We judge others according to results; how else?—not knowing the process by which results are arrived at. If Miss Tulliver, after a few months of well-chosen travel, had returned as Mrs Stephen Guest—with a post-marital trousseau and all the advantages possessed even by the most unwelcome wife of an only son, public opinion, which at St. Ogg's, as elsewhere, always knew what to think, would have judged in strict consistency with those results.

. . .

But the results, we know, were not of a kind to warrant this extenuation of the past. Maggie had returned without a trousseau, without a husband—in that degraded and outcast condition to which error is well known to lead; and the world's wife, with that fine instinct which is given her for the preservation of society, saw at once that Miss Tulliver's conduct had been of the most aggravated kind. (*The Mill on the Floss*, bk 7, chap. 2)

In 1854 Lewes and Marian, after telling only a few friends of their plans, embarked publicly on their unorthodox relationship. They did so out of England. As Lewes needed to visit Weimar and Berlin to research his life of Goethe, it was to Weimar that they went together in July 1854, Marian sending her famous telegram on 19 July to Charles and Cara Bray and Sara Hennell:

> Dear Friends—all three
>
> I have only time to say good bye and God bless you. Poste Restante, Weimar for the next six weeks, and afterwards Berlin. (*Letters*, 2.166)

While acquaintances in London and Coventry discussed the liaison (with Chapman and Bray joining in the head-shaking and moralizing), Marian and Lewes settled down to hard work and social pleasure at Weimar. Lewes worked on his biography of Goethe, helped in the translation of extracts by Marian. She also spent time translating Spinoza's *Ethics*, a work which, with its stress on man's self-love being naturally balanced by the love of society and a natural sympathy with others of his species, was at least as influential on George Eliot's own humanism as were Feuerbach's and Comte's versions of the religion of humanity. Unfortunately, Lewes quarrelled with the publisher Bohn on their return to England about the financial terms for Marian's translation, which remained unpublished until 1981.

In Weimar the Leweses met the composer Franz Liszt, who was living with a married woman without raising eyebrows. Marian and Lewes, too, were able to go about together without shocking anyone. But on their return to England in March 1855, Marian found that she was no longer accepted in mixed society. She and Lewes found lodgings first at Clarence Row, East Sheen, then at 8 Park Shot, Richmond, where they remained until February 1859, by which time George Eliot had sprung on the world with the publication of *Scenes of Clerical Life* in 1858 and the extremely successful *Adam Bede* in February 1859. Their male friends from the *Westminster Review* circle visited, of course, as before, but did not bring their wives. Marian had to tell her enthusiastic feminist friend Bessie Parkes to address letters to Mrs Lewes, not Miss Evans, so as not to arouse the suspicion of the landlady. Lewes was invited out to dinner, but not Marian.

In 1856 Marian, encouraged by Lewes, first tried her hand at fiction. Despite the anonymity of her journalism, she was already well known in London's literary circles as the author of several trenchant articles and reviews in the *Westminster Review* on a variety of subjects, including the writing of fiction. In her article 'The natural history of German life' (July 1856) she advocated a particular (Spinozan) kind of realism in art: 'The greatest benefit we owe to the artist, whether painter, poet, or novelist, is the extension of our sympathies'; and 'Art is the nearest thing to life; it is a mode of amplifying our experience and extending our contact with our fellow-men beyond the bounds of our personal lot' (*Essays*, 270–71). These remarks read like a manifesto for the kind of fiction she was very soon to write herself.

One of the last articles Marian wrote for Chapman before beginning 'The Sad Fortunes of the Reverend Amos Barton', the first of the three stories which made up *Scenes of Clerical Life*, was a sparklingly witty attack on the 'left-handed imbecility' of certain minor female novelists. Called 'Silly novels by lady novelists', and published in the *Westminster Review* in October 1856, it divides the novels according to certain classes: 'the *mind-and-millinery* species', 'the *oracular* species', and 'the *white neck-cloth* species'. This last type represents evangelicalism, a subject Marian knew much about from her early life as well as from her wide reading. She criticizes those contemporary novelists who mix evangelical religion with high society. 'The real drama of Evangelicalism', she writes, 'for any one who has genius enough to discern and reproduce it—lies among the middle and lower classes' (*Essays*, 318). Whereupon she set about showing how it could, and should, be done.

The emergence of
George Eliot

First novels

Partly because of her anomalous social position, and partly because she had always liked to work anonymously, Marian Evans chose to write under a pseudonym. In November 1856 Lewes sent the manuscript of 'Amos Barton' to the Edinburgh publisher John Blackwood, saying it was by a 'shy, ambitious' friend of his (*Letters*, 2.269, 276). No name was given for this unknown author, and Blackwood actually began corresponding, via Lewes, with 'My Dear Amos'. He knew he was dealing with a potentially great writer, telling his mysterious correspondent in January 1857 that he had recently confided to William Thackeray that he had 'lighted upon a new Author who is uncommonly like a first class passenger' (ibid., 2.291). Marian replied to this praise on 4 February 1857, signing herself for the first time George Eliot. The name was chosen, as she later told John Cross, because George was Lewes's forename and Eliot was 'a good mouth-filling, easily pronounced word' (Cross, 1.431).

Other Victorian women published under male pseudonyms: most famously, the Brontë sisters had published their works in the 1840s under the names Currer, Ellis, and Acton Bell. But it would be wrong to think that women found it necessary to hide behind a masculine name in order to be published and appreciated. Novel writing had long been recognized as a genre suitable for women to write—particularly the novel of social manners, a subject which they could be expected to know about. Fanny Burney and Maria Edgeworth had written under their own names at the beginning of the century, and Elizabeth Gaskell was happy to write her novels without recourse to a pseudonym.

But Marian Evans was known as the freethinking radical of the *Westminster Review*, the 'strong-minded woman', as Carlyle called her (*Letters*, 2.176n.), and the woman who was living with a married man. She needed the protection of a pseudonym. It also suited her constitutional diffidence and fear of failure to conceal her identity, as it had suited her to be the unnamed though independent and managing editor of Chapman's *Westminster Review*. Moreover, once it was known that George Eliot was Marian Evans, or Mrs Lewes, the pseudonym endured, in contrast to the Bell pseudonyms of the Brontës. One probable reason for this was the difficulty her contemporaries experienced in addressing or naming the author—was she to be called Miss Evans, or Mrs Lewes? The pseudonym solved the problem. Another reason may be the strong narrative voice of George Eliot, with its echoes of the genial, man of the world tone of a Fielding or a Scott, together with the range of reference employed by a narrator who seems equally *au fait* with the domestic (and hence usually female) and the public and professional (usually male) spheres.

The three stories which together make up *Scenes of Clerical Life*—'The Sad Fortunes of the Rev. Amos Barton', 'Mr Gilfil's Love Story', and 'Janet's Repentance'—have some awkwardness of structure. Their slow expositions, intended to embody George Eliot's Wordsworthian view that there is abundant passion and interest in ordinary working lives, are followed by hasty, even melodramatic conclusions. But with their deft contextualizing and strong dialogue, they indicated the arrival of a fresh new talent among Victorian writers of fiction. The *Scenes of Clerical Life* were published serially in *Blackwood's Magazine* from January to November 1857, often appearing on facing pages with Lewes's lively work of popularizing marine biology, *Sea-Side Studies*, which was being serialized at the same time. Marian was paid £260 for the serialization in *Blackwood's*, and £180 for the separate publication in book form which followed in 1858 (*Letters*, 7.359–60). Meanwhile, she had taken the decision to tell her family in Warwickshire of her new life with Lewes. She wrote to her brother Isaac, who, when he ascertained that her marriage was not a legal one, instructed his solicitor to inform his sister that he wished to have no more contact with her. He prevailed on their sister Chrissey and half-sister Fanny to stop corresponding too. It was a blow to Marian's feelings, although she was not surprised at Isaac's disapproval, having encountered it at the time of losing her faith and again when she made the move to London.

Encouraged by the success of her three clerical stories, Marian soon set about writing her first full-length novel, *Adam Bede*, which brought her instant fame on its publication in February 1859. Dickens admired it (and guessed the author was a woman); Elizabeth Gaskell was flattered to be asked if she had written it. The novel evokes pastoral romance and the picturesque qualities of country life around 1800, while at the same time embodying George Eliot's ideas of realism as expounded in her essays and in *Scenes of Clerical Life*. She catches the ugliness as well as the beauty, the unkindness as well as the neighbourliness, of country life. A conventional story of the seduction of a young country woman, Hetty Sorrel, by the squire in waiting, Arthur Donnithorne, is handled in a distinctly unconventional way, with several chapters devoted to the pregnant Hetty's lonely and desperate journey in search of her lover. Also, unusually, George Eliot wins the reader's interest for her saintly heroine, Dinah Morris, the Methodist preacher modelled in some respects on Marian's aunt Elizabeth Evans, wife of her father's brother Samuel, who had converted to Methodism as a young man.

Criticism and acclaim

Inevitably, gossip got to work, both in London's literary circles, where Herbert Spencer let out the secret of the authorship, and in Warwickshire, where readers, including members of Marian Evans's estranged family, recognized characters and settings in both *Scenes of Clerical Life* and *Adam Bede*. Authorship was claimed for a midlands man called Joseph Liggins, who, although he himself never went into print on the subject, allowed others to do so without refuting the claim. The 'Liggins business' lasted for two years, with letters being written in *The Times* and the pro-Liggins faction, which included Mrs Gaskell, refusing to accept Blackwood's public statements denying that Liggins was the author. The business of keeping her identity secret, although important to the sensitive Marian, caused her anguish, and the persistence of the Liggins myth, combined with the rumours of literary London, led her at last to admit defeat and allow it to be known, in June 1859, that George Eliot was Marian Evans, alias Mrs Lewes.

Marian's friends were, on the whole, pleased, although Sara Hennell felt jealous and suddenly left behind by a friend now departed into 'glory', and Herbert Spencer also showed resentment at his friend's tremendous success (*Letters*, 3.49n., 95–6). Cara Bray, who had taken a long time to accept the liaison with Lewes, wrote warmly congratulating her friend, and robust feminist friends like Bessie Parkes and Barbara Bodichon were jubilant both at her success and at the discomfort of those who disapproved of her life.

On discovering the identity of George Eliot, many readers and critics were shocked to find that the novelist they had welcomed for her humanity, her humour, her tolerance, and the moral— though neither moralistic nor religious—ethos of her work was none other than the freethinking, free-loving (as the caricature of her relationship with Lewes went) Marian Evans. In due course society adjusted to the shock of finding that one of its greatest writers was an unbeliever and a woman in a compromising social position. By the time George Eliot's sixth and greatest novel, *Middlemarch*, had appeared in 1871–2, her status as England's finest living novelist was assured.

But at the time of *Adam Bede* itself, Marian found that her enjoyment of its success—with accolades in all the journals and sales of more than 10,000 copies in the first year, well beyond her, or Blackwood's, wildest dreams—was soured by the Liggins problem and the uproar in some quarters which followed on the lifting of the veil of anonymity. Only Lewes's encouragement and cheerfulness and Blackwood's firm and friendly support—he sent her an extra £400 for *Adam Bede* on top of the £800 he had originally paid for it, in order to give her a fair share in its unexpected success—kept her from giving up fiction and even, according to Lewes in September 1859, leaving England altogether to get away from the 'fools' who 'obtrude themselves upon her' (*Letters*, 8.245). Marian's debt to Lewes is eloquently expressed on the manuscript of the novel (now in the British Library), which she dedicated to him: 'To my dear husband, George Henry Lewes, I give this M.S. of a work which would never have been written but for the happiness which his love has conferred on my life.'

The Mill on the Floss

The painfulness of having her domestic situation discussed and judged by all and sundry finds indirect expression in 'The Lifted Veil', an uncharacteristically gloomy, even morbid, tale of second sight and hatred which Marian wrote early in 1859, as *Adam Bede* was being published to acclaim and work on her next novel, *The Mill on the Floss*, had begun. Both the short story and the new novel bear witness to the distress and depression against which Marian was struggling, despite her domestic happiness with Lewes and her success as a novelist. The miracle is that *The Mill on the Floss*, with its tragic plot based on the loving yet mutually thwarting relationship between Tom and Maggie Tulliver, and its bold approach to the difficulties of sexual attraction, should also be such a humorous work. It is evidence of Marian's ability—seen in miniature in the comic letter to Bray in 1846—to turn painful personal experience to comic, as well as tragic, account.

During the writing of this novel Marian learned that her sister Chrissey was dying of consumption. In February 1859 Chrissey wrote, regretting the break in their relations. She died on 15 March. It is hardly surprising that Marian's bitter feelings towards Isaac find expression in some harsh authorial remarks about Tom Tulliver in *The Mill on the Floss*. Family life had been a battle for her; she had been at odds with her father and brother, and estranged from Chrissey, though they had been close and Marian had helped her sister financially on the death of her husband in 1852, when Chrissey had been left with six young children and little money. *The Mill on the Floss* illustrates in several of its relationships the remark made by the narrator of *Adam Bede*: 'Nature, that great tragic dramatist, knits us together by bone and muscle, and divides us by the subtler web of our brains; blends yearning and repulsion; and ties us by our heartstrings to the beings that jar us at every movement' (chap. 4). Yet *The Mill on the Floss* is also full of the rich comedy of family life as represented mainly by the three Dodson aunts of Tom and Maggie. The novel's form displays on a fictional level the serious intellectual engagement that she had with the nineteenth-century debate on evolution—Darwin's *On the Origin of Species* was published late in 1859, only a few months before *The Mill on the Floss* appeared.

With *Adam Bede*, George Eliot had become a best-selling author. Accordingly, Blackwood offered her

£2000 for her second novel, with a royalty of more than 30 per cent (Haight, *Biography*, 318). *The Mill on the Floss* was published in April 1860, and within four days had sold 4600 copies. By the end of 1860 it had earned Marian the impressive amount of £3865 (*Letters*, 7.360). Marian and Lewes had gone abroad on an extended trip to Italy late in March to avoid the inevitable comments on the recently revealed identity of the author. They visited all the major Italian cities; in Florence, Lewes drew Marian's attention to the history of the city in the late fifteenth century, particularly the role in public life played by the Dominican monk Savonarola, who led a religious revival after the fall of the Medici family but was tried and executed as a heretic in 1498. In due course George Eliot was to base her historical novel *Romola* (1863) on his story.

In June 1860 Marian and Lewes travelled to Hofwyl in Switzerland, where Lewes's three sons, Charles, aged nearly eighteen, Thornie, aged sixteen, and Herbert, aged fourteen, were at school.

They brought Charles back to London with them; he studied for the civil service exams and took up a job as clerk in the Post Office. Because of the inconvenience for Charles of travelling to work daily from the Leweses' home in Wandsworth, they moved into London, first in September 1860 to 10 Harewood Square, near Regent's Park, then round the corner to 16 Blandford Square in December. Gradually, Marian began to go out to concerts, theatre, and dinner-parties, finding that she was becoming more welcome in general society than she had been on her return from Germany with Lewes in 1855. Samuel Laurence painted her portrait, completing it in September 1860. Lewes did not like it, but Blackwood, recognizing the 'sad pensive look' which had struck him when he first met her, bought it to hang in his office in Edinburgh (*Letters*, 3.343).

Silas Marner and *Romola*

George Eliot's next work was the short novel *Silas Marner*, begun in November 1860, and finished in March 1861. She experienced much less depression and fewer delays than was usual for her in its composition. With its happy ending, its legendary plot of the miser who turns into a philanthropist and finds happiness in adopting a child, it is different from her other novels, while sharing their humour and breadth of understanding. Though contemporary readers were, on the whole, fondest of *Adam Bede* among her novels, the response to *Silas Marner* was gratifyingly warm. Eight thousand copies were sold by the end of 1861, bringing her £1760 (Haight, *Biography*, 341).

By contrast, *Romola* proved the most difficult novel to write and in the long run the least popular of George Eliot's works. It was certainly the one on which she laboured for longest and not, it must be admitted, to altogether happy effect. *Romola* was thoroughly researched for (too much so, according to Lewes and to many readers and critics), both in Italy and in the reading room of the British Museum, but the writing went slowly and by fits and starts. The resulting novel, though full of fine things, is too cramped, crowded, and laborious to come to life imaginatively. It falls short, in places, of George Eliot's own requirement, artic- ulated in a letter of 1866, that 'aesthetic teaching', 'the highest of all teaching because it deals with life in its highest complexity', should never lapse 'from the picture to the diagram' (*Letters*, 4.300).

While Marian was writing *The Mill on the Floss*, relations with her supportive publisher John Blackwood had become strained. She felt he had not done enough to dispel the Liggins myth and feared, not without justification, that he was nervous about the public response to that novel now that the identity of George Eliot was widely known. When George Smith, a London publisher with money to spare and a new journal, the *Cornhill Magazine*, to launch, offered Lewes the editorship of the journal and George Eliot an unprecedented £10,000 to publish *Romola* in twelve monthly parts in the *Cornhill*, beginning in July 1862, she accepted, though with a bad conscience. Trying to keep up with the relentless pace of part publication proved a nightmare for her. The novel also fell rather flat with critics and the public. Though Marian voluntarily took £7000 rather than the offered £10,000, Smith still lost money on it. She felt guilty towards him for his loss and also towards Blackwood for having deserted him.

Later years and writing

Life at The Priory

The Leweses, now comfortably off thanks to
Marian's earnings, searched for a larger house.
They found The Priory near Regent's Park.
Lewes's friend, the designer Owen Jones (chief
designer of the Crystal Palace), was commissioned to decorate the living rooms at consider-
able expense, and in November 1863 the Leweses
moved in and entered on a splendid style of living.
Here at The Priory they soon began to hold regular Sunday afternoon parties for friends and vis-
itors, including Darwin, Huxley, Spencer, Henry
James, and the artist Frederic Leighton, who illustrated *Romola*.

At last the Leweses were being invited out together by literary friends and admirers. Although it was not until 1877 that Marian was introduced to royalty in the person of Queen Victoria's daughter Princess Louise, the queen herself had read all of George Eliot's novels, admiring *Adam Bede* so much that in 1861 she had commissioned Edward Henry Corbould to paint two scenes from the novel—one of Dinah Morris preaching, the other of Hetty Sorrel making butter in the dairy.

In 1865 Frederic Burton drew Marian's portrait, which he gave to the National Portrait Gallery in 1883. Friends reckoned that this was the best likeness of the few she allowed to be taken. Like Laurence's, it shows a melancholy long-faced woman with abundant brown hair and intelligent but sad eyes. Contemporaries who saw her agreed with her own estimate of her appearance as plain (and many enjoyed noticing that Lewes, too, was ugly); Henry James summed it up best, perhaps, when he wrote to his brother William in 1878: 'The great G.E. herself is both sweet and superior, and has a delightful expression in her large, long, pale equine face' (Ashton, *George Eliot*, 275).

As agitation grew during 1866, leading finally to the passing of the second Reform Act of 1867, George Eliot returned for her next novel to England and to the familiar midlands countryside of her early novels. *Felix Holt, the Radical* (1866) takes for its subject and milieu the upheavals of society at the time of the first Reform Act of 1832. She once more approached her old publisher John Blackwood, who responded with warmth to her return, offering her £5000 for the copyright for five years (Haight, *Biography*, 384). Blackwood appreciated, as did her readers, the richly observed social scene, although the election riot on which the plot turns, based in part on a polling-day riot which occurred in her native Nuneaton in 1832, is a rather tame affair, and Felix Holt himself is unconvincing both as a radical and as a hero. There is also an over-elaborate mystery about exchanged identities and legal arrangements of estates, not unlike that in Dickens's most recent novel, *Our Mutual Friend* (1865) and in Wilkie

Collins's works. *Felix Holt* was less successful than *Adam Bede*, *The Mill on the Floss*, or *Silas Marner*, although nearly 5000 copies were sold in the first year (ibid., 387).

In December 1866 Marian and Lewes visited Spain. Lewes's health was poor, and the journey was gruelling, but both had long wished to see Granada and the Alhambra. While on this visit, Marian had the idea of writing about the expulsion from Spain of the Moors and the Gypsies in the 1490s, and the result was *The Spanish Gypsy* (1868). The Gypsy of the title, Fedalma, has to choose between duty to her race and love of a Catholic duke. As with *Romola*, the conception and execution are less than successful, the more so as, after some deliberation, she cast this story in the form of a dramatic poem in blank verse. One of her most sympathetic and astute critics, Richard Holt Hutton, noticed that 'verse to her is a fetter, and not a stimulus'; Henry James asked readers to imagine what it would be like if Tennyson wrote a novel or George Sand a tragedy in French alexandrines (Ashton, *George Eliot*, 294).

Though the response to *Romola*, *Felix Holt*, and *The Spanish Gypsy* was polite, Marian was aware of a drop in her popularity. She could not know that her next work, an amalgam of two stories begun and abandoned, would be acclaimed her masterpiece. It was the result of a brilliant idea to knit together her story about the arrival of a young doctor in a midlands town shortly before the Reform Act of 1832 and a second story, 'Miss Brooke', about the marriage choice of an idealistic young woman of the landed gentry.

Middlemarch was not, however, written under the most auspicious circumstances. During its slow production Marian battled against self-doubt and illness. Not only did she suffer from the usual agonies of composition; she and Lewes spent the summer of 1869 nursing Lewes's second son, Thornie, through the excruciatingly painful illness of tuberculosis of the spine, of which he finally died, aged twenty-five, in October 1869. The irrepressible Thornie had failed his civil service examinations in 1863 and had gone out to

Africa to farm. The venture, undertaken with his younger brother Herbert, was not wholly successful financially, and Thornie had contracted his fatal illness in Natal. Lewes sent him money to take the passage home, in the hope that he might be cured in England. Instead, he came home to die.

By May 1871 it was clear to Marian and Lewes that *Middlemarch* was becoming too long to fit the usual three-volume format. Lewes suggested to Blackwood that, on the model of Victor Hugo's *Les misérables*, it should be brought out in eight parts at two-monthly intervals, and subsequently published in four volumes. This mode of publishing was duly adopted, and the novel appeared to public delight from December 1871 to December 1872. About 5000 copies of these 5s. parts were sold. By 1879 nearly 30,000 copies had been sold in one edition or another, earning Marian about £9000. This astonishingly fully realized 'study of provincial life'—the subtitle of the novel—brought the author admiring reviews and letters from friends and strangers enthusing about her

understanding of human life, male and female,
rich and poor, professional and domestic, married
and unmarried, happy and unhappy.

In *Middlemarch*, the social changes of the early
1830s are thoroughly absorbed into the multiple
plot connections between individuals—what the
narrator calls 'the stealthy convergence of human
lots' (chap. 2). And George Eliot shows more than
ever before her ability to enter imaginatively into
the consciousness of every kind of human being,
from the naive, aspiring Dorothea Brooke to the
petrified pedant Casaubon, from the ambitious
Dr Lydgate to his ill-matched unresponsive wife,
Rosamond, from the loud merchant and mayor
Vincy to his brother-in-law, the evangelical banker
Bulstrode. The portrayal of the two unhappy mar-
riages, the Lydgates' and the Casaubons', drew
praise from Freud; Henry James wrote of the
'painful fireside scenes between Lydgate and his
miserable little wife' that there was 'nothing more
powerfully real' and 'nothing certainly more *intelligent*' in all English fiction (Ashton, *George Eliot*,
325).

On a visit to Germany in the summer of 1873 the Leweses visited the spa town of Bad Homburg. There they witnessed a scene of international gambling at the casino which was to provide material for the striking opening of George Eliot's next and last novel, *Daniel Deronda*. Like *Middlemarch*, it appeared in eight parts, this time monthly during 1876. While creating once more a panorama of social classes and opinion and showing how individuals interact at times of social change, this novel spreads its net even wider than its predecessor, taking in the English aristocracy at one end of the scale and poor London Jews at the other end. George Eliot's ambitious plot brings the two extremes into close contact through the figure of Deronda himself; her comic treatment of the ludicrous hunting and shooting county set is daringly offset by her respectful description of the Jewish religion and culture embodied in the ailing scholar Mordecai.

Marian was aware, as she admitted in April 1876, that 'the Jewish element' would be 'likely to satisfy nobody' (*Letters*, 6.238). Certainly, though the novel sold well, and earned its author over £9000, and though Blackwood, while not keen on the parts exclusively concerned with Mordecai's philosophy and vision of a Jewish homeland, saw that the work was full of brilliance, critics were puzzled, praising the 'English' parts for the familiar humour and insight, while they felt awkward about the 'Jewish element'.

There are a number of possible reasons why George Eliot turned to the vision of a Jewish homeland. By *Middlemarch* she had gone as far as it was possible to go in the imaginative study of English provincial life. Marian's wide intellectual curiosity, in evidence from her earliest years through her learning of foreign languages, translations of Spinoza, Strauss, and Feuerbach, and critical appreciations of Goethe, George Sand, and other European authors, and reinforced in recent years by frequent visits abroad, led her to set the scene of *Daniel Deronda* partly outside England. She had become interested in Judaism, through her friendship with Emanuel Deutsch, an orientalist employed by the British Museum, who taught her Hebrew. Deutsch had a vision of a Jewish homeland in the East; he travelled to Palestine, and died in Alexandria in 1873. Marian sympathized with his idealism, and was also irritated by the routine antisemitism she encountered among her acquaintances. She told Blackwood that she had wanted in *Daniel Deronda* to 'widen the English vision a little' (Ashton, *George Eliot*, 348).

Marian was exhausted at the end of writing another long novel. In November 1876 she and Lewes found a country house, The Heights, in Witley, near Haslemere in Surrey, which they bought with a view to spending the summers there. But they were to enjoy only two idyllic summers, and even those were overshadowed by anxiety about Lewes's failing health. He died of enteritis and cancer on 30 November 1878, aged sixty-one, and was buried in the dissenters' part of Highgate cemetery on 4 December. Marian was too distraught to attend. She was plunged into loneliness, filling her journal with verses from

Tennyson's great poem of mourning, *In Memoriam* (1850), as Queen Victoria had also done after the death of Prince Albert.

Marriage and death

Without Lewes to help, Marian was unable to decide whether to publish her rather heavy and subdued set of ironic character sketches, *Impressions of Theophrastus Such*, which Blackwood eventually brought out in 1879. She spent her time preparing the last two volumes of Lewes's five-volume work of physiology and psychology, *Problems of Life and Mind* (1874–9), for the press, and arranging for the founding of a George Henry Lewes studentship in physiology at the University of Cambridge. For months she would not see her friends, even the adoring younger women Edith Simcox and Elma Stuart, who had attached themselves to her in recent years. She could bear to be visited only by Lewes's one remaining son Charles and by the friend who had found the house at Witley for them, the banker John Walter Cross.

Cross's mother had died within a few days of
Lewes. He, a bachelor of forty who had lived
with his mother and sisters, needed consolation
too. Several months later he asked Marian, more
than twenty years his senior, to marry him. She
hesitated, still devastated by the loss of Lewes and
acutely aware of the great age difference, but in
the spring of 1880 she agreed to marry Cross.
Despite her lack of religious affiliation, and pre-
sumably in deference to the Cross family, they
were married in St George's, Hanover Square,
on 6 May 1880. Charles Lewes gave her away.
She and Cross went on their honeymoon to Italy,
leaving behind a startled public and some disap-
proving friends. She now reverted to her childhood forename, calling herself Mary Ann Cross,
and seemed destined to shock once more with
the last great decision of her life. If the orthodox
had shaken their heads at the 'elopement' with
Lewes, both they and the non-orthodox found
it hard to adjust to her sudden marriage to a
man much younger than herself. One positive—
if meagre—result was a brief letter of con-
gratulations from her estranged brother Isaac,

content that his wayward sister, whom he had always known as Mary Ann, was now legally married.

Mary Ann's happiness was short-lived. Cross became depressed on the honeymoon and fell, or threw himself, from the balcony of their Venice hotel into the Grand Canal. Though little is known about the details of his illness, it fuelled gossip at home, with many a club-going acquaintance of Cross's commenting on both the age gap and the intelligence gap between husband and wife. According to Edith Simcox, whose autobiography is one of the few sources of information about Cross, he had suffered from bouts of depression before his marriage (Ashton, *George Eliot*, 377).

Back home by the end of July, the Crosses went to Witley to recuperate. Mary Ann suffered from recurring kidney trouble. On 3 December 1880 they moved into their splendid new house, 4 Cheyne Walk, by the Thames at Chelsea. Less than three weeks later, on 22 December, she died of the kidney disease she had suffered from for several years, exacerbated by a throat infection.

Cross inquired about the possibility of burial in Westminster Abbey, where Dickens and other great writers had been buried. Herbert Spencer was among those who thought that George Eliot, too, should have her place in Poets' Corner. But many felt that her denial of Christian faith, as well as her 'irregular' (though monogamous) life with Lewes, ruled this out. Cross dropped the idea, and on 29 December she was buried instead alongside Lewes in the dissenters' part of Highgate cemetery. It was fitting that she should be laid to rest beside the man who had cherished her and encouraged her genius, overriding her tendency to paralysing self-doubt and despondency. But it was also fitting that in 1980, 100 years after her death, a memorial stone was finally established in Poets' Corner, so that this great writer should be seen to be honoured in the same way as others who have enriched, as she undoubtedly did, the national literature.

George Eliot was one of the greatest Victorian writers. Recognized as such in her lifetime, when, like Dickens, she was both an admired and a commercially successful novelist, she suffered a temporary decline in reputation in the decades following her death. This was largely due to her husband's well-meaning but misguided efforts, in the biography he published in three volumes in 1885, to portray her as respectable despite her unorthodox relationship with Lewes. Cross, who had only got to know her in 1869, when she was fifty, who was in awe of his famous older wife, and who was, in addition, not a natural writer, gave a picture of her as a stuffy, sibylline figure. Not only did he silently change passages in her letters, removing her trenchancy, her 'salt and spice', as Hale White noticed, but he omitted much, including the whole history of her relationship with Chapman. Cross may also have destroyed the pages of George Eliot's journal relating to her life in London up to the journey to Germany with Lewes. The extant journals, which remained unpublished until 1998, begin in July 1854, with evidence that the first forty-six pages have been removed (Haight, *Biography*, xv).

Everything that was unusual, strong-minded, and racy about her was left out of the picture, and by the 1890s George Eliot was being described as a heavy, humourless writer. For example, in 1890 the critic W. E. Henley characterized her—surely without having read the novels—as 'George Sand *plus* Science and *minus* Sex' (Carroll, 42). Leslie Stephen was an honourable exception to the general depreciation of her; he wrote an admiring volume on her in the (in this case ironically named) English Men of Letters series in 1902, and he was the author of the sympathetic entry on George Eliot in the first edition of the *Dictionary of National Biography* (1888).

It was Stephen's daughter Virginia Woolf who began the true rehabilitation of George Eliot's reputation with an essay in the *Times Literary Supplement* in 1919, the centenary of George Eliot's birth, in which she famously remarked that *Middlemarch* was 'one of the few English novels

written for grown-up people' (Carroll, 43). There-
after George Eliot was influentially praised by
F. R. Leavis in *The Great Tradition* (1948); and
with the great biographical and editorial work
done by Gordon Haight in his nine-volume edition of her letters (1954–5, 1978) and his thorough
documentary biography (1968), appreciation of
George Eliot's greatness, and interest in all aspects
of her life and work, were restored.

The last decades of the twentieth century saw all
George Eliot's works republished, and her journals and working notebooks published for the first
time. All the novels are available in paperback,
and *Middlemarch* in particular is taught on many
school and university English literature courses.
Although not so frequently adapted for radio, television, and film as Dickens's, George Eliot's novels
have had some notable BBC television adaptations:
Daniel Deronda in 1970 and 2002, *Silas Marner*
in 1985, and *Middlemarch* in 1994. The *Middlemarch* production resulted in paperback editions
of the novel entering the best-seller lists for the
first time since the novel's original publication,

making George Eliot once more that rare phenomenon, a novelist whose success can be measured in both sales figures and critical esteem.

Appreciation

Marian's was a difficult life, but a brave and extremely interesting one. Curious, sceptical, critical, and even rebellious by nature, she was also timid, self-doubting, longing to conform where she felt compelled to rebel. This complex and conflicting combination of traits can be seen in all the important relationships of her life: with her father Robert Evans, her brother Isaac, the partner of her life, G. H. Lewes, and John Walter Cross, her husband of a few months. The combination can also be seen, duly transformed by her extraordinary imaginative and narrative gift, in the ambitious handling of human problems in her novels, where she skilfully, sympathetically, and wittily puts difficult choices before her characters, showing their frailty in both comic and tragic mode and analysing their often mixed and confused motives.

As a novelist George Eliot managed to be both a moralist and a realist. She appreciated in Goethe's novel *Wilhelm Meister's Apprenticeship* his honesty in depicting 'irregular relations in all the charms they really have for human nature', while also representing 'every aspect of human life where there is some trait of love, or endurance, or helplessness to call forth our best sympathies' (*Essays*, 145, 146). Art should extend our sympathies by opening our imaginations to understand unheroic, even dislikeable, characters like Mr Casaubon and Mr Bulstrode, even while we judge their faults. It was George Eliot's special gift to apply her wide knowledge, penetrating analytical intelligence, and humorous sympathy to the depiction of characters, their motivation, and their interaction in a densely realized social milieu. All her novels illustrate the famous remark made by the narrator in *Felix Holt*: 'There is no private life which has not been determined by a wider public life' (chap. 3). She experienced as much in her own unusual life, which became so cosmopolitan from unpromising provincial beginnings, and so adventurous intellectually and socially—particularly for a woman in the nineteenth century—after a timid, conventional early life. Yet she delved deep into that provincial and conventional past for much of the material—the felt life—which animated her fiction. As Lewes remarked in 1873 to a Coventry friend of Marian's early years, 'she forgets nothing that has ever come within the curl of her eyelash' (Ashton, *George Eliot*, 205). All the phases of her experience, from piety to scepticism, from family life to social exile, from provincial obscurity to professional fame, with the pleasures and pains associated with families and small communities and associated also with expulsion, exile, or escape from them, are absorbed by the philosophical intelligence, literary allusiveness, and strong sense of dialogue and structure in those fine novels of George Eliot.

Sources

The George Eliot letters, ed. G. S. Haight, 9 vols. (1954–78) · G. S. Haight, *George Eliot: a biography* (1968) · R. Ashton, *George Eliot: a life* (1996) · J. W. Cross, ed., *George Eliot's life as related in her letters and journals*, 3 vols. (1885) · R. Ashton, *G. H. Lewes: a life* (1991) · R. Ashton, 'New George Eliot letters at the Huntington', *Huntington Library Quarterly*, 54 (1991), 111–26 · *Essays of George Eliot*, ed. T. Pinney (1963) · *Selected critical writings*, ed. R. Ashton (1992) · D. Carroll, ed., *George Eliot: the critical heritage* (1977) · G. S. Haight, *George Eliot and John Chapman: with Chapman's diaries* (1940); 2nd edn (1969) · W. H. White, 'George Eliot', *The Athenaeum* (28 Nov 1885) · C. Bray, *Phases of opinion and experience during a long life* (1884) · L. Stephen, *George Eliot* (1902) · F. R. Leavis, *The great tradition* (1948)

Index

The finest scholarship on the greatest people...

Many leading biographers and scholars have contributed articles on the most influential figures in British history: for example, Paul Addison on Winston Churchill, Patrick Collinson on Elizabeth I, Lyndall Gordon on Virginia Woolf, Christopher Ricks on Alfred Tennyson, Frank Barlow on Thomas Becket, Fiona MacCarthy on William Morris, Roy Jenkins on Harold Wilson.

'Paul Addison's Churchill ... *is a miniature masterpiece.'*

Piers Brendon, *The Independent*

Every story fascinates...

The *Oxford DNB* contains stories of courage, malice, romance, dedication, ambition, and comedy, capturing the diversity and delights of human conduct. Discover the Irish bishop who was also an accomplished boomerang thrower, the historian who insisted on having 'Not Yours' inscribed on the inside of his hats, and the story of the philanthropist and friend of Dickens Angela Burdett-Coutts, who defied convention by proposing to the Duke of Wellington when he was seventy-seven and she was just thirty. He turned her down.

'Every story fascinates. The new ODNB will enrich your life, and the national life.'

Matthew Parris, *The Spectator*

www.oxforddnb.com

At 60,000 pages in 60 volumes, the *Oxford Dictionary of National Biography* is one of the largest single works ever printed in English.

The award-winning online edition of the *Oxford DNB* makes it easy to explore the dictionary with great speed and ease. It also provides regular updates of new lives and topical features.

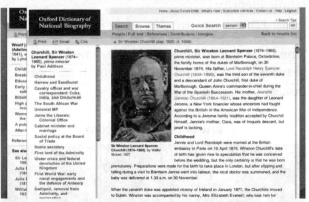

www.oxforddnb.com

The *Oxford Dictionary of National Biography* was created in partnership with the British Academy by scholars of international standing.

It was edited by the late Professor H. C. G. Matthew, Professor of Modern History, University of Oxford, and Professor Sir Brian Harrison, Professor of Modern History, University of Oxford, with the assistance of 14 consultant editors and 470 associate editors worldwide.

Dr Lawrence Goldman, Fellow and Tutor in Modern History, St Peter's College, Oxford, became editor in October 2004.

What readers say

'The *Oxford DNB* is a major work of reference, but it also contains some of the best gossip in the world.'

John Gross, *Sunday Telegraph*

'A fine genealogical research tool that allows you to explore family history, heredity, and even ethnic identity.'

Margaret Drabble, *Prospect*

'The huge website is superbly designed and easy to navigate. Who could ask for anything more?'

Humphrey Carpenter, *Sunday Times*

www.oxforddnb.com